Lifesize Ocean

Written by Anita Ganeri
Illustrated by Stuart Jackson-Carter

KINGFISHER
NEW YORK

KINGFISHER

LONDON & NEW YORK

Copyright © Kingfisher 2014
Published in the United States by Kingfisher,
175 Fifth Ave., New York, NY 10010
Kingfisher is an imprint of
Macmillan Children's Books, London.
All rights reserved.

Consultant: Steve Savage
Editor: Clare Hibbert
Design and styling: Maj Jackson-Carter
Cover design: Mike Davis

Distributed in the U.S. and Canada
by Macmillan, 175 Fifth Ave.,
New York, NY 10010

Library of Congress Cataloging-in-Publication data
has been applied for.

ISBN: 978-0-7534-7096-1 (HB)
ISBN: 978-0-7534-7097-8 (PB)

Kingfisher books are available for special promotions and premiums. For details contact:
Special Markets Department, Macmillan, 175 Fifth Ave., New York, NY 10010.

For more information, please visit www.kingfisherbooks.com

Printed in China
1 3 5 7 9 8 6 4 2
1TR/0114/WKT/UG/128MA

Contents

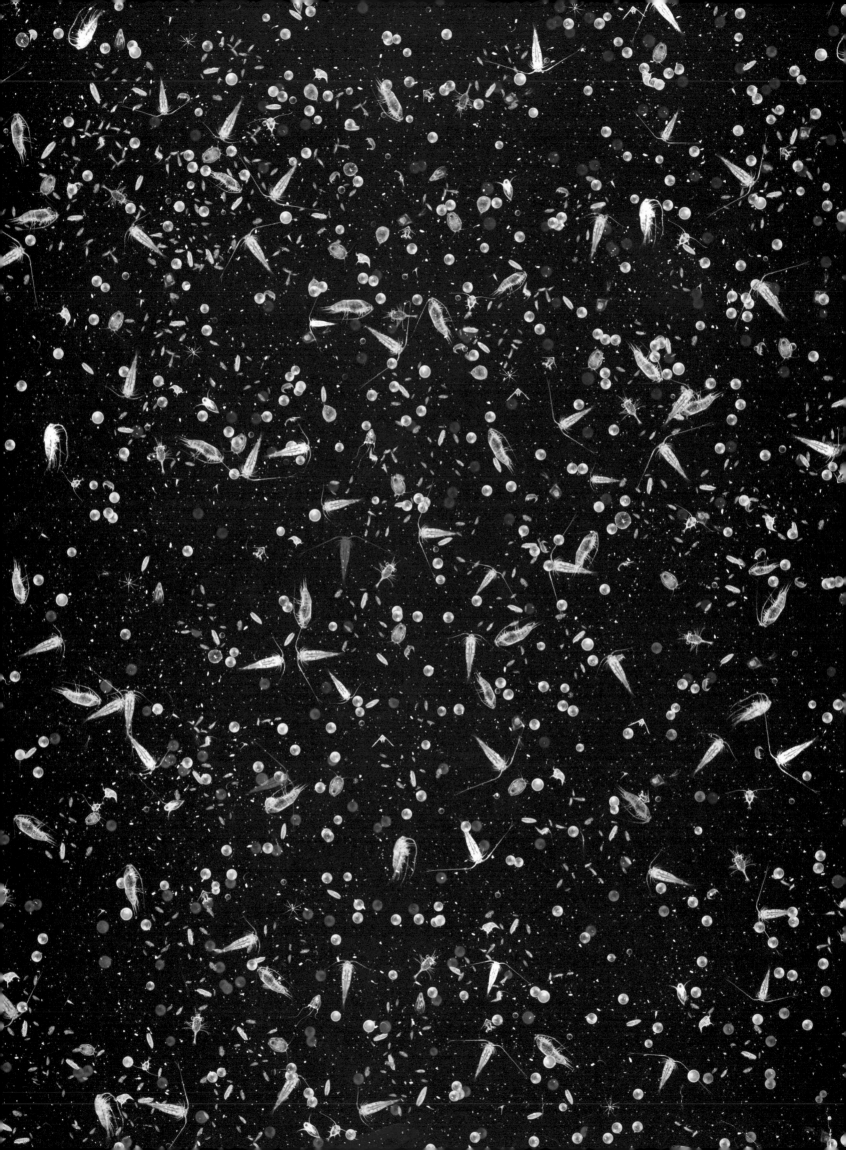

Copepods

Drifting in the ocean is a soup of teeny-tiny plants, eggs, and animals. This soup, known as plankton, includes copepods—teardrop-shaped creatures with trailing antennae. Copepods are crustaceans, related to lobsters and crabs. They sweep tiny plants into their mouths with special feeding legs.

Pygmy seahorses

How many pygmy seahorses are in this picture? Look carefully—they are hard to spot! Not only are these amazing animals small, they are also fantastically camouflaged. Pygmy seahorses live only on sea fans, a type of coral. They match the coral perfectly, even down to their lumps and bumps.

Turn to page 32 to check how many seahorses are in the picture.

Scarlet skunk cleaner shrimp

A moray eel stops to be cleaned. This usually ferocious fish stays very still as a team of scarlet skunk cleaner shrimp gets to work. The shrimp scurry all over its body, picking parasites and dead scales off its skin and gills. They even venture inside the eel's mouth to nibble pieces of leftover food from its sharp teeth!

Blue-ringed octopuses

Two blue-ringed octopuses prowl the reef, on the lookout for crabs and fish. These delicate creatures are small and usually shy. But they are also some of the deadliest animals in the ocean, capable of killing a human in minutes with a single, venomous bite.

Black devil anglerfish

In the dark, deep ocean, a female anglerfish lurks. She has a
long fin, like a fishing rod, with a glowing blob of light at the
end. When prey comes close, attracted by the light, her gaping
mouth snaps shut. This anglerfish must nourish both herself
and her much smaller mate, who clings to her belly by his teeth.

Long-spined porcupine fish

Faced with a hungry predator, a porcupine fish gulps in water and blows itself up to twice its usual size. The long, sharp spines on its body stick up, making it too big and prickly a mouthful for any attacker. Once the danger has passed, the fish shrinks back to normal, its spines flat against its skin.

Sea otters

A sea otter mother and her pup doze in the water, wrapped in strands of seaweed to keep them from drifting away. When she wakes, the mother dives for mussels, clams, and sea urchins. She lies on her back and smashes the shellfish against a rock balanced on her chest to get to the meat inside.

Green sea turtle

Using its front flippers as paddles, a green sea turtle powers through the water, occasionally surfacing to breathe. It spends most of its life at sea, but females come ashore to lay their eggs. When the babies hatch, they must dash to the ocean or risk being eaten by hungry gulls and ghost crabs.

19

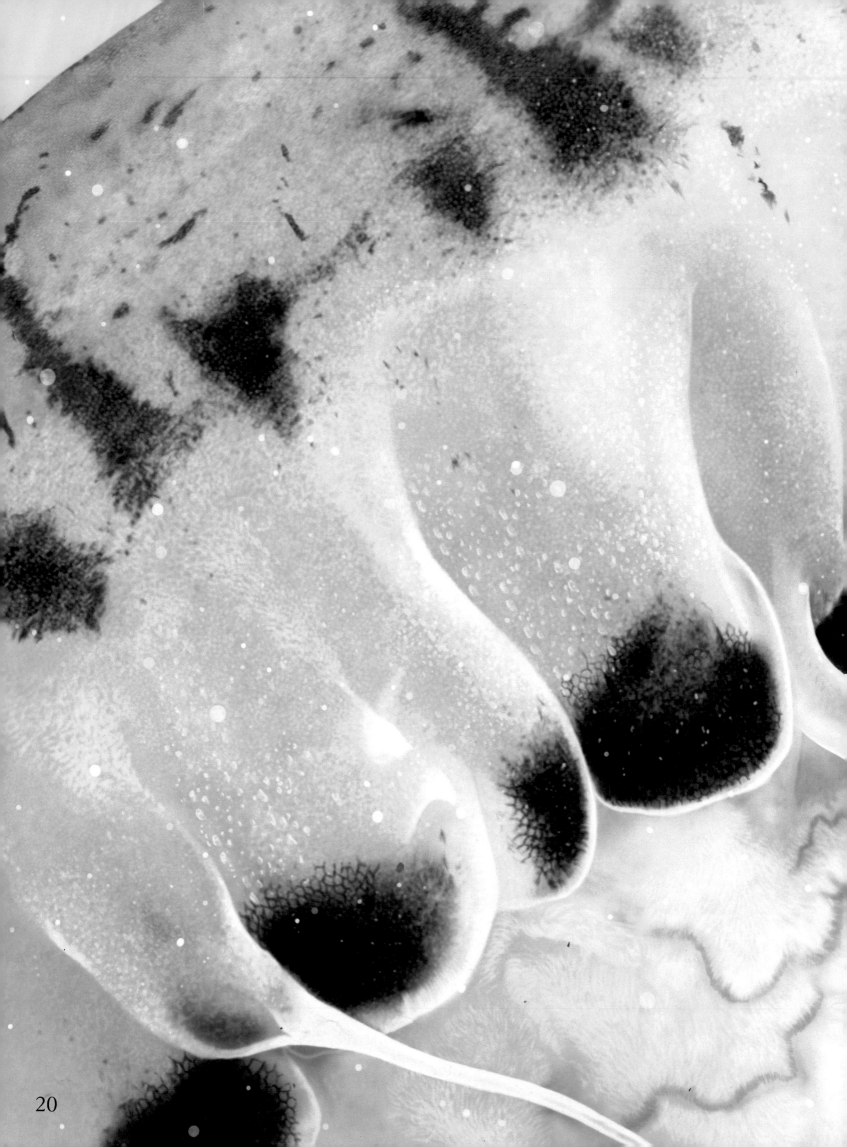

20

Purple-striped jellyfish

With its bright stripes, this giant jellyfish is a striking sight—but it is also armed and dangerous! It trails long tentacles covered in stinging cells. They stun or kill any copepods or other prey that brush past them, and then the jellyfish can pull its meal into its mouth.

Great hammerhead shark

A great hammerhead scans the water for stingrays, its favorite food. The shark's odd, hammer-shaped head has special sensors that pick up electrical signals from a ray buried in the sand. The shark can use the side of its head to pin down its prey so that it can't escape. Then the hunter bites off big chunks of the ray's flesh.

23

Giant Pacific octopus

As night falls, a giant Pacific octopus leaves its den to go hunting. Each of its eight arms is as long as a human diver and studded with suckers. The octopus stalks or chases its prey. Its beaklike mouth can bite open crab or mollusk shells or drill a hole for sucking out the insides.

Blue whale

Everything about a blue whale is ENORMOUS, from eyeballs as big as grapefruits to a heart the size of a small car. Its favorite things to eat are tiny, shrimplike creatures called krill. The whale gulps in a huge mouthful of water, sifts out all of the krill, squirts out the water, and then swallows the krill.

Animal facts

Most copepods have a single, bright red eye on their head.

Copepod

Habitat: Oceans around the world

Length: 0.04–0.2 in. (1mm–5mm)

Weight: Less than 0.00004 oz. (1mg)

Diet: Phytoplankton (tiny plants) and zooplankton (tiny animals)

Average lifespan: Less than a year

Amazing fact: Copepods use their long antennae to detect food and enemies. They can tell which is which by sensing the way water flows around their bodies.

Like all octopuses, the blue-ringed octopus has three hearts and blue blood.

Scarlet skunk cleaner shrimp

UNDER THREAT

Habitat: Coral reefs in the Indian and Pacific oceans

Length: Up to 2.5 in. (6cm)

Weight: Not known

Diet: Parasites, dead skin, and fungi

Average lifespan: 3–5 years

Amazing fact: The shrimp's bright colors make them easy to spot at their cleaning stations. They also wave their antennae and do a special dance to attract passing fish.

UNDER THREAT

Blue-ringed octopus

Habitat: Reefs and rock pools around Australia and the western Pacific Ocean

Length of body: 2 in. (5cm)

Length of tentacles: 2.75–3 in. (7cm–7.5cm)

Weight: Around 57 lb. (26kg)

Diet: Crabs, fish, and mollusks

Average lifespan: 2 years

Amazing fact: The octopus has a pattern of 50–60 rings on its body. When it is alarmed, the rings glow bright blue, warning that the octopus might bite.

The shrimp is named after the white stripe down its back, like a skunk's.

Pygmy seahorses curl their tails around sea fans to avoid being swept away.

UNDER THREAT

Pygmy seahorse

Habitat: Coral reefs in the western Pacific Ocean

Length: Up to 0.75 in. (2cm)

Weight: Not known

Diet: Tiny shrimp and other crustaceans

Average lifespan: 12–18 months

Amazing fact: Male seahorses have babies. The male carries the eggs in a pouch on his front until they hatch. Then up to 30 tiny babies shoot out and swim away.

UNDER THREAT

Animals are under threat if their numbers are falling and they risk becoming extinct (dying out forever). Or they may be under threat because their habitat is disappearing.

Black devil anglerfish

Habitat: Deep ocean (2,300–5,000 ft., or 700m–1,500m) around the world

Length: Up to 7 in. (18cm) (female); up to 1 in. (3.5cm) (male)

Weight: Up to 21 oz. (600g) (female; male not known)

Diet: Fish, crustaceans, squids, and worms

Average lifespan: Not known

Amazing fact: The female anglerfish's "fishing rod" fin glows because of millions of light-making bacteria.

An anglerfish's pitch-black skin camouflages it in the dark water.

Sea otter

Habitat: Kelp forests in the north Pacific Ocean

Length: 3–5 ft. (1m–1.5m)

Weight: Around 66 lb. (30kg)

Diet: Sea urchins, mollusks, and crustaceans

Average lifespan: 15 years

Amazing fact: Sea otters are sometimes seen in large groups, called "rafts." A raft can contain hundreds of otters. Being in a group helps protect them from attack by sharks and killer whales.

Long-spined porcupine fish come out to hunt at night.

Long-spined porcupine fish

Habitat: Coral reefs, mangrove swamps, and muddy flats around the world

Length: Up to 20 in. (50cm)

Weight: Not known

Diet: Mollusks, sea urchins, and hermit crabs

Average lifespan: 5–8 years

Amazing fact: The long-spined porcupine fish uses its hard, beaklike mouth to crack open mollusk shells.

Sea otters can close their nostrils and ears in the water.

UNDER THREAT

Green sea turtles have green fat underneath their shells.

Purple-striped jellyfish

Habitat: Open waters off the California coast, Pacific Ocean

Diameter of bell (body): Up to 3 ft. (1m)

Length of tentacles: Up to 16 ft. (5m)

Weight: Not known

Diet: Copepods, jellyfish, and fish eggs

Average lifespan: Not known

Amazing fact: Young purple-striped jellyfish don't have purple stripes. They have pale pink bells and long, dark red tentacles. They change color as they get older.

Green sea turtle

Habitat: Tropical oceans around the world

Length: Up to 5 ft. (1.5m)

Weight: Around 287 lb. (130kg)

Diet: Algae and seagrass

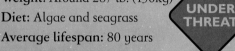

UNDER THREAT

Average lifespan: 80 years

Amazing fact: Green sea turtles travel long distances to breed. Some swim more than 1,250 mi. (2,000km) from Brazil to tiny Ascension Island in the middle of the Atlantic Ocean.

Some crabs live inside purple-striped jellyfish and feed on harmful parasites.

Blue whales have superloud voices! They can hear one another from 1,000 mi. (1,600km) away—unless other sounds, such as boat engines, get in the way.

Hammerheads give birth to litters of up to 40 pups.

Giant Pacific octopus

Habitat: Coastal areas of the north Pacific Ocean

Arm span: Up to 16 ft. (5m)

Weight: Up to 110 lb. (50kg)

Diet: Crustaceans, mollusks, and small fish

Average lifespan: 3–5 years

Amazing fact: When an octopus is alarmed or disturbed, it can activate special cells in its skin and change color from reddish-brown to white or red.

Female giant octopuses lay strings of 20,000–100,000 eggs.

Great hammerhead shark

UNDER THREAT

Habitat: Open and coastal waters around the world

Length: Up to 20 ft. (6m)

Weight: Up to 1,000 lb. (450kg)

Diet: Stingrays and other fish, squids, and octopuses

Average lifespan: 20–30 years

Amazing fact: Great hammerheads' heads are 24–35 in. (60cm–90cm) wide. When hunting at dawn and dusk, they swing their heads back and forth to pick up signals from their prey.

Blue whale

UNDER THREAT

Habitat: Oceans around the world (except the Arctic)

Length: Up to 100 ft. (30m)

Weight: Up to 220 tons (200 metric tons)

Diet: Krill

Average lifespan: 80–90 years

Amazing fact: Blue whales give birth to babies that are already 23 ft. (7m) long and weigh more than 2.2 tons (2 metric tons). By drinking its mother's rich milk, a baby whale can double its weight in a week.

Saving ocean animals

All over the world, oceans and their wildlife are in danger from pollution, oil and gas drilling, global warming, and overfishing. Scientists, conservation groups, and governments are working hard to learn more about the oceans so that they can find better ways to take care of them. One plan is to turn parts of the ocean into parks where animals and plants are protected. The Great Barrier Reef off the coast of Australia is already a marine park.

Why are green sea turtles in danger?

Many are caught for their meat and eggs.

Others die after swallowing plastic.

Thousands more get tangled in fishing nets and drown.

Five groups working to save ocean animals:

Greenpeace works to protect the environment. It is campaigning for more marine parks and less harmful ways of fishing. www.greenpeace.org

The Nature Conservancy works with the fishing industry, local communities, and governments to develop fishing programs that keep ocean habitats healthy. www.nature.org

Oceana campaigns to protect oceans from pollution and overfishing. It persuades governments around the world to help preserve marine life and habitats. www.oceana.org

The Pew Charitable Trusts, through its Global Shark Conservation campaign, is working to reverse the decline of shark populations. www.pewtrusts.org

The Sea Turtle Conservancy was set up to stop sea turtles from becoming extinct. It tracks individual turtles by satellite. www.conserveturtles.org

Answer: There are 16 pygmy seahorses in the picture on pages 6 and 7.